CONTENTS

► A lizard scampers across desert sand (see page 12).

THE DRY ZONE

Deserts are places that get very little rain. Some deserts are without any rain for years at a time. All living things need water to survive, so deserts are one of the hardest places on Earth to live.

You can tell when you are in a desert because most of the landscape is bare of plants. Many deserts have hot weather and are sandy, like vast beaches. The sand may form huge mounds called sand dunes. But most hot deserts are rocky and stony. The Earth's polar regions are cold, icy deserts.

Most hot deserts are in lands near the Equator. The sky overhead is usually clear, with no clouds to shade the ground. During the day the Sun beats down, making the ground scorching hot. But when the Sun sets, the ground soon cools down, so the nights are very cold.

▲ These sand dunes are in the Sahara Desert in north Africa. The dunes change shape as the wind blows the sand about.

▶ Wind and sand wear away desert rocks into strange shapes. An arch is made when the softer centre of a rock is weathered away.

A desert might look empty of life, but it may be home to many kinds of plants and animals. Some people, too, live in the desert or spend time there. These plants, animals and people are adapted to, or have developed, ways of surviving in the desert's extreme conditions.

DISAPPEARING RAIN

Some deserts are so hot, any rainfall dries up before it reaches the ground. Heat from the ground changes the falling drops of rain into water vapour or steam.

NORTH AMERICA

Sonora Desert

EUROPE

ASIA

Gobi Desert

Thar Desert

Sahara Desert

Arabian Desert

AFRICA

Equator

SOUTH AMERICA

Atacama Desert

Kalahari and Namib Deserts

Gibson Desert and The Outback

AUSTRALIA

Hot deserts

Hot deserts – the focus of this book – cover about a fifth of all the land in the world. Those mentioned in this book are labelled.

ANTARCTICA

GETTING DRIER

When you travel towards a desert, plants become scarcer. First, most of the trees disappear, leaving low bushes. The bushes in the semi-desert grow farther and farther apart until you reach the desert itself.

Deserts are getting bigger. The semi-desert is turning into desert and grasslands are becoming semi-desert. One reason is that the world is becoming warmer and less rain is falling. Also, people living in the semi-deserts cut down bushes for firewood, and their goats and sheep eat the plants faster than they can regrow.

In some places, people try to stop the desert spreading. They plant acacia trees and bushes that grow well in dry places. The trees and bushes grow fast and provide the people with firewood and food for animals.

▲ Hungry goats like these are one of the reasons semi-deserts are becoming deserts. Goats devour plants.

Even in deserts, there are places where you can find water. Such a place is called an oasis. The water is below the ground. Sometimes it bubbles to the surface and forms a pool. Elsewhere, people dig a well to reach it. Wherever they can, people use the water to irrigate the land to grow crops.

▲ This town in Morocco is built around an oasis. It provides water for plants, animals and people.

SPREADING DESERTS

Every year deserts and semi-deserts grow bigger. Up to 135 million people around the world may soon have to leave their land because it will be too dry to farm.

▼ These barriers of twigs and branches will stop the soil blowing away. The roots of plants also help to keep any soil in place.

QUICK CHANGES

Desert plants and animals have to survive extreme changes. Each day the temperature changes from very hot to very cold. It seldom rains but when it does, it pours, causing flooding.

In the heat of the day, when the temperatures may rise to 45°C, most animals hide under stones or in burrows. At night the temperature plummets to below freezing (0°C). Soon after sunset, animals leave their shelters to look for food. Desert people, too, often rest by day and travel at night. They find their way by the stars.

▼ After rain, the desert floor blooms. In this semi-desert in Mexico, gold poppies appear among the cactuses.

TRICK OF THE LIGHT
Sometimes desert travellers think they see water where there is none. This is called a mirage. Light from a patch of sky is bent so that the patch of sky looks like water on the ground.

Some desert plants and animals rest both night and day for months on end. They are waiting for rain. When enough water falls, they spring into life. Flowers bloom and quickly make seeds. The eggs of desert shrimps and frogs hatch and adults lay more eggs. When the rain dries up, these seeds and animals lie dormant again until the next downpour.

One of the harshest times to be in a desert is during a sandstorm. Strong winds whip up sand and dust into a thick cloud. People cover their faces and skin to protect themselves from the flying sand.

▲ Spadefoot toads, like this one in Arizona, USA, spend most of their lives underground. They surface when it rains to lay their eggs, which hatch into tadpoles like these.

◄ A sandstorm blows across the desert in Saudi Arabia. The wind can carry the sand for hundreds of kilometres.

DESERT PLANTS

Desert plants have developed special ways of surviving with almost no water. They have also found ways to defend themselves against hungry desert animals.

Desert plants have long roots to suck in as much water as possible. Some have roots that probe deep into the ground to reach water far below. Others have roots that spread out to collect water from a wide area. A few desert plants even take in dew through their leaves.

Once a plant has taken in water, it stores it. Some plants store water in their roots. Others have thick, juicy leaves. Cactuses have no leaves. Instead they store water in their tough, swollen stems. The stored water keeps the plant alive when its roots cannot find water in the soil.

▼ Trees that grow among rocks, as here in Joshua Tree National Park, California, have deep roots as well as wide-reaching, shallow roots. The deep roots anchor the tree in soil under the rocks.

WEIRD WELWITSCHIA

Welwitschia grows in the Namib Desert, southern Africa. It has two long, straggling leaves that with age split along their length. Their job is to channel dew into the ground to feed the plant's thick roots.

▼ *Welwitschia* lives for 100 years or more. Its leaves can grow to 18m, but wind damage usually keeps them nearer 3m long.

To protect themselves from being eaten, Prickly pears and other cactuses are covered with sharp spines. Some cactus spines are poisonous and shaped like fish-hooks to dig into an animal's flesh. Stone plants disguise themselves by looking like pebbles. Most of the plant is hidden under the ground, safe from animals and the heat.

◄ Prickly pear cactus grows well in deserts. Its roots reach down more than 10m. This cactus is in Arizona. It has several flowers.

SMALL CREATURES

Deserts are home to an amazing variety of small animals – insects, scorpions, reptiles and small mammals. They have all found ways of coping with the extreme desert conditions.

Many insects, especially those without wings, come out to hunt at night. They drink the dew that collects in the cold night air. Some beetles do headstands, so the dew runs down their backs into their mouths!

▲ A scarab beetle helps to recycle dung. It lays its eggs in a pellet of dung, which provides food and moisture for the grubs when they hatch.

▲ If you saw this lizard in the desert, you might think it was dancing. When it walks, it quickly lifts each leg in turn to avoid burning its feet on the hot sand.

Reptiles, such as lizards and snakes, use the heat of the Sun to warm their bodies. At midday they shelter under rocks or burrow in the sand to escape the searing heat. Reptiles can last a long time without food. Most hunt when the ground cools, but some lizards are active during the day. They run fast so they do not scorch their feet.

Small mammals spend the day in underground burrows and come out at night to look for food. Gerbils, hamsters and Kangaroo rats feed on seeds. The rats use their long back legs to jump out of the way of predators, such as snakes or the small desert fox.

NOT A DROP TO DRINK

Kangaroo rats live in the deserts of the south-western United States. They manage to live on hardly any water, because they lose none from their bodies. They never sweat and their urine is almost solid.

▼ Only its snout and eyes give away this snake, hidden in the Namibian sand. It is ready to strike any prey that comes by.

BIG BEASTS AND BIRDS

Large animals need more water and food than small animals. Even so, animals such as camels, antelopes and kangaroos are all at home in a desert habitat.

Few large animals live in the desert all the time. Jackals are wild dogs that venture into the Kalahari Desert to hunt. Red kangaroos and gazelles move into desert areas only when the scrubby semi-desert is overcrowded. Oryxes, however, are antelopes that spend their lives in the Arabian Desert. They get enough water from the grasses, bulbs and roots that they eat.

▼ The cactus wren nests in the Saguaro cactus. Its scaly legs protect it from the spines.

◀ Red kangaroos can survive in the Australian deserts.

▶ A camel's body is well-adapted to desert life.

Body temperature rises during the day and falls at night to avoid sweating and chilling.

Hair protects the skin during the day and gives warmth at night.

Long legs keep body well above the hot ground.

Broad, flat feet do not sink in the sand.

Camels can go for days without food and water, but when they come to an oasis they can quickly gulp down as much as 100 litres of water. A camel has a bulky body with one or two humps on its back. The humps are stores of fat, which the camel draws on when it is short of food.

LONG LASHES

A camel has long, curling eyelashes to protect its eyes from sand, and thick eyebrows to shade them from the Sun. Its ears are lined with hairs that keep out the sand.

Many desert birds fly high in the sky during the day to escape the desert heat. But the Sand grouse hardly moves in daylight. It feeds on grass and seeds and waits until dusk or dawn to fly to its watering holes.

OASIS LIFE

Oases (plural of oasis) are amazing. Palm trees, grass and bushes grow in the middle of a bare desert. An oasis can be small, or supply a whole city with water.

Sometimes rainwater trickles through gaps in rocks and becomes trapped in an underground lake. This lake might be under a desert, many kilometres from where the rain originally fell. If the desert is low-lying, or there is a fault in the rock, the water forms a pool on the surface. Otherwise, people bore a well to reach the water.

▼ Palm trees grow alongside an oasis in Sudan from which water is piped to an adjoining vegetable garden and nearby mudbrick house.

EXTRA WATER

In the United States, Phoenix and Las Vegas are desert cities. They started as towns built on oases. To allow the towns to grow into cities, in the 1930s the Roosevelt and Hoover Dams were built to supply extra water.

◀ Wells provide water for cattle as well as people. This well in Kenya has a ditch alongside for the animals.

Wherever there is fresh water, plants can grow. Desert people grow crops, especially date palms, for food and shade. The trees also provide wood for building and burning. Toads, snakes, birds and other animals live among the plants around an oasis, feeding on the plants or the insects they attract.

▲ This desert hotel in Tunisia is built under the ground to keep the rooms cool in the scorching heat.

In the Sahara and Arabian Deserts, people build houses of mud around small oases. Mud bricks are cheap and easy to make. They keep the houses cool during the day and warm at night. People who live near an oasis have to be careful not to use too much water, or the oasis will run dry.

DESERT HUNTERS

At one time, many people lived in deserts. For food, they hunted animals and gathered plants. Today, only a few people in southern Africa and Australia still do this.

Desert hunters are always on the move. They do not plant crops, keep animals or have permanent homes. The San people live in the Kalahari Desert in southern Africa. They build shelters from grass and branches of trees. The women collect berries, seeds, nuts and roots and the men hunt.

▼ This San hunter is about to shoot an ostrich with a bow and arrow. The hunter often puts poison on the tips of the arrows.

▼ The traditional San home is a grass shelter. These San are making arrows for hunting.

A few Australian Aboriginals still live as desert hunters. They build grass shelters and gather plants and small animals to eat. In the past, all Aboriginals were constantly moving, looking for water and food. The men hunted kangaroos and other game using spears and boomerangs.

THE SHOSHONI

The Shoshoni lived in what is now Nevada, Idaho and Utah in the USA. They moved through the desert searching for seeds, roots and small animals. They planned their journeys to reach each source of food when it was most plentiful.

Today, only a few San people and Aboriginals follow a traditional way of life. Most live in towns or work on farms. Examples of their art and culture remain, however. In the Kalahari, you can still see San rock paintings made thousands of years ago. Aboriginals, too, created rock paintings, carvings and other art.

▲ Traditionally, Aboriginals hunted with spears and boomerangs. The boomerang was thrown to hit an animal and stun it.

NOMADIC HERDERS

Many people who live in the desert are nomadic herders. They have to keep moving from place to place to find enough plants for their animals to eat.

Nomads do not plant crops. Instead they keep herds of animals. The Bedouin travel the deserts of North Africa and the Middle East. Their sheep and goats provide them with milk, meat and wool. They make tents out of woven goat hair. They also keep camels to carry goods and to sell.

In Kenya, the Turkana are nomads for half the year. In the dry season, they travel with their herds of cows, sheep and goats in search of good pasture. When the rains come, they settle for a while and grow crops.

▼ The Turkana build their temporary homes from palm fronds. Here, a Turkana husband and wife stand outside their home.

Nomads in Mongolia have to survive cold winters, as well as hot desert conditions. They live in yurts – tents made from felt or hides – that keep out the heat in summer and the cold in winter. Mongolian nomads use ponies as well as camels to transport their goods. They keep herds of sheep for food and wool.

WASHING UP WITH SAND

Desert nomads do not waste precious water washing dirty dishes. Instead they clean them by rubbing them in the sand. See how well this works by rubbing a penny in the sand. It will come up sparkling clean!

▲ Men and women who live in hot deserts dress in long, loose clothes. Their clothes protect them from the Sun and wind.

▼ In Mongolia, nomadic people usually ride ponies rather than camels. Camels are more likely to spit and be bad-tempered!

DESERT TRAVELLERS

Today, many people use cars and other vehicles to drive across a desert. Deserts are dangerous places. All travellers must prepare carefully before they start on their journey.

FLASH FLOODS

One of the great dangers in the desert is flash flooding. After a thunderstorm in the mountains, desert canyons and riverbeds may be suddenly awash with fast-flowing water. This sweeps away rocks, stones – and any people or vehicles.

Some people go into the desert for an adventurous holiday. Other people drive across the desert simply to reach somewhere on the other side. In the United States, ordinary cars drive across the desert on tarmac roads. Where there are no roads, drivers need to use four-wheel-drive (4WD) vehicles.

▲ The banks of this riverbed in Grand Canyon National Park, Arizona, have been quickly washed away by a sudden downpour. The water is thick with sand.

Desert travellers should always tell someone where they are going and how long they will take. They must pack drinking water – at least 4 litres a day for each person. Bottled water, or boiled and cooled tap water, is best. They also need to take sufficient fuel and water for their vehicle.

To protect themselves from the Sun, travellers should wear a broad-brimmed hat and clothes that cover their bodies. They should find out what snakes live in the desert and take some antivenin just in case of a bite. They may also need protection against biting insects, such as mosquitoes.

▲ This truck stirs up a huge cloud of dust as it travels across the dry, dirt road in the semi-desert of the Australian Outback.

▼ Riding a camel is one of the best ways to travel across the rocky deserts of North Africa.

STRANDED!

Even well-planned journeys can go wrong. People who travel across the desert must know what to do if they have an accident or their vehicle breaks down.

Travellers need to know how to repair their vehicle. The engine may overheat or a tyre may burst. Driving over sand, wheels can become stuck. They turn in the loose sand, but do not move forward. The best way to get the vehicle moving again is to dig the sand away and put boards or sacks under the wheels.

SIGNALLING FOR HELP

Helicopters are often used to look for people who are lost in the desert. People who need help can signal by making a large triangle on the ground from newspapers or tinfoil. A triangle is a recognized distress signal.

▲ In Morocco, the driver of this car is letting some air out of the tyres. Softer tyres give better grip on loose sand.

People stranded in the desert should stay with their vehicle and wait. If they told someone of their plans, that person will raise the alarm. Rescuers will soon be on their way.

The most dangerous problem is thirst. If people do not have enough water to last until they are rescued, their bodies become dehydrated. Their mouths become dry and swollen. After a while they may begin to see things that are not there – a mirage. They may think that they can see an oasis and start to walk towards it. With no water, most people will die after a few days.

▲ Even a tarmac road can quickly disappear under the sand. Giant barriers like this keep the road free of sand.

▼ Travelling by camel in Mongolia has its advantages – a camel will not break down or become stuck in the sand. But it does need food and water.

DESERTS: FACTS

SIZE OF DESERTS

The world's largest desert is the Sahara in North Africa. It covers 9 000 000 sq km – about the same size as the United States. Deserts in North America cover 1 300 000 sq km, an area twice the size of Texas.

EXTREME HEAT

Death Valley in California is the hottest place in the United States. In summer the air temperature often rises to 52 °C. The ground becomes even hotter – up to 80 °C.

OSTRICHES

Ostriches live in the deserts in Africa. They are the world's largest bird. At about 2.4m, they are taller than people. Ostriches cannot fly but they can run very fast – at up to 64 km/h.

LACK OF WATER

The Atacama Desert in Chile, South America, is the driest place on Earth. It gets an average of less than 0.1 mm of rain each year and has not had a good downpour of rain for more than 20 years.

▼ Various kinds of snakes are found in both deserts and semi-deserts. They are well-adapted to the hot, dry conditions.

TALLEST CACTUS

A Saguaro cactus can reach 18m high. Its stems can store up to 8 tonnes of water. It is covered with a waxy layer to keep water in and to protect the plant from the Sun.

HIDDEN SUPPLIES OF WATER

In the past, each group of San people roamed over a particular area of desert. They knew the land well, especially sources of underground water. They would stick a hollow reed into the ground and use it like a straw to suck up the water.

DISTRESS SIGNALS

A triangle on the ground is an accepted distress signal, or call for help. There are other distress signals too. An L means that someone is injured. An F means that you need food and water. An X means that you are stuck.

◀ The Saguaro grows only in the desert in southern Arizona, south-eastern California and northern Mexico.

DESERTS: SUMMARY

Deserts present living things with extreme conditions ranging from scorching daytime temperatures and lack of water to scarcity of food.

Plants such as cactuses store water and have no leaves that lose moisture to the air. Animals, including lizards and snakes, use the heat to warm up their bodies. Then they shelter from the sun. Goats eat almost any kind of food they can find. People can survive in deserts only if they keep cool during the day, warm at night, and have a plentiful supply of drinking water. Disturbance or pollution of deserts by tourists, trekkers, farmers, foresters, city- and airport-builders damages this environment.

▼ Rolling dunes in the Sahara Desert form a sea of sand. Crossing the Sahara is as hazardous today as it has been for thousands of years.

DESERTS: ON THE WEB

You can visit deserts on the Internet. Use a search engine and type in the name of the desert you want to find out about, or the desert animal or plant. Here are some good sites to start with:

Deserts of the World
www.factmonster.com/ipka/A0778851.html
This web page has lots of information about all of the world's deserts.

Desert Life
www.desertusa.com
Learn what a desert is and how many there are in North America. Explore the plant and animal life, the environment and geology, as well as the people and cultures.

The Sahara
www.calacademy.org/exhibits/africa/exhibit/
    sahara/
This website tells the story of the Sahara Desert — why it formed and what it is like now.

Desert Museum
http://desertmuseum.org/kidz/index.html
This website is from Arizona's Desert Museum. There is information about the Sonora Desert and the unusual creatures and plants that live there.

Desert Survival
www.ci.phoenix.az.us/FIRE/desert.html
Information about surviving in hot and cold desert conditions, including what to do if you get lost and how to signal for help.

▼ **Many desert towns are full of surprises. Here storks have built huge nests on the rooftops of a fortress in west Africa.**

DESERTS: WORDS

This glossary explains some of the words used in this book that you might not have seen before.

Antivenin
treatment against the venom (poison) in the bite or sting of a snake, spider or scorpion.

Crops
plants grown for food.

Dam
a wall that is built to block a river and form a lake.

Dehydrated
drying out due to lack of water.

Dew
drops of water that form on the ground or on leaves at night as the air cools.

Dormant
inactive as though sleeping.

Equator
an imaginary circle drawn around the centre of the Earth.

Fault
a crack or break in rocks caused by movements under the Earth.

Flash flood
a sudden rush of water that fills a riverbed or stream bed.

Grasslands
an area in which the main plants that grow are grass and only a few trees.

Irrigate
water the land for crops.

▼ A camel rests, close to the desert pyramids in Egypt.

Nomadic
moving around to find water and food for oneself and one's animals.

Oasis
a place in the desert where there is water. Plants such as date palms often grow around an oasis.

Predator
an animal that hunts other animals for food.

Prey
an animal that is hunted by another animal.

Reptile
an animal that has a scaly skin. Reptiles include snakes, lizards and tortoises. Reptiles cannot make their own heat and have to asbsorb warmth from their surroundings.

Roots
the part of a plant that grows in the soil. Roots take in water and help to anchor the plant.

Sand dune
a mound or hill made of sand.

▲ These towers of weathered rock stand like guards in the desert in Western Australia.

Scorpion
a relative of spiders with four pairs of legs and pincers. It has a sting at the end of its tail that it uses mostly for defence.

Semi-desert
countryside with few plants that is almost or partly desert.

Survive
to stay alive

Urine
yellow liquid waste that leaves the body through the kidneys and bladder.

Watering hole
a place where water is found, for example at an oasis.

Well
a natural or artificial hole that reaches underground water.

INDEX